Basement Sentiment: Poetry from the Dark

Kate Phillips

BookLeaf Publishing

India | USA | UK

Basement Sentiment: Poetry from the Dark
© 2024 Kate Phillips

All rights reserved.

Kate Phillips asserts the moral right to be
identified as author of this work.

Presentation by *BookLeaf Publishing*

Web: www.bookleafpub.com

E-mail: info@bookleafpub.com

ISBN: 9789363313378

First edition 2024

*For my beloved canine companion
Beauregard, to all the bright places we're
going*

ACKNOWLEDGEMENT

Thank you to my friends and family who have been supportive of my work

Thank you to my parents for the opportunities they've given me and for always doing their best

Thank you to Lorejean Ramirez for reliably picking up the phone

Thank you to Kyrstyn Kelly, my pig-hearted friend for never letting me be alone

Thank you to Bea Ortilla, my dog's god mother, for your dedication to our friendship

Thank you to Charles Wolgemuth for your daily creative input and support

Thank you to Jennifer McCumber for being there when I need you and for being the prettiest girl in the whole entire world

A special thank you to Jacob Buzby for being my best friend and inspiration to embrace the good things

And thank you to me, for choosing to write this
book instead of rotting. Keep going.

PREFACE

The poems in this book are a tribute to the darkest moments of my life. It is from healing and growth beyond those moments that allowed me to continue to write. It is my greatest hope that I never again come so close to death. But when I do, I will find peace in knowing that I lived my life with authentic resilience.

Trust Me

Silken paws meet soft snow

They have never known such cold –

It is instinct to play.

Winter falls on busy souls

Darkened doorways,

Stories told

A young dog, ever bold

Curiosity –

Held captive prey

Sunflowers

My flowers feel no guilt
I've known them since they were small

I read to them at night
They've gotten very tall

Sometimes I'll sit out with them
Stretching towards the sun

I tell them that I love them
I tell them that they're fun

My flowers have grown freely
Something I have never done

Mental

Months feigning silence
Worried to be found

Only to discover
impenetrable sound

Secure in your prison
Emaciated hound

Desire to speak freely
But to your secrets I've been bound

Thinker's Prize

Be wary of the Thinker's lair—

His tricky darkened down.

His hoard resides in shadows—

His thinking is not sound.

One by one,

The Travelers come,

To win the Thinker's prize.

And one by one,

Each Traveler's Sun,

Sets his own demise.

Now I am wary of the Thinker's lair—

Escaping once with help.

But now I cannot help but think—

Of ways to escape myself.

Risk

In the dark
The silence screams

Daylight chirps behind
Blackened blinds

I feel the walls
Wheeze as they weep

Clever mouse
Warm in his sanctity

Lays among hunters
Fed in the dark

Terrible Secret

I can keep a secret
Tell me all of yours

Thought I could keep a secret
Should have known there would be more

You'd rather remain anonymous
Than a spectacle deplored

Your secrets weigh like burdens
But I keep all of yours

Lukewarm

Your torrid taunting

Hid ornate affairs –

Clandestine conspiracy

Provokes mental warfare –

Your conscience expunged,

Without guilt you confess –

You're a stranger to love,

But not a stranger to death.

Method Actor

I practiced my smile a hundred times,

Adding counterfeit emotion to lines—

Sixty-dollar smog hangs in the air,

The choice isn't yours,

This doesn't feel fair—

Don't cause a scene,

They're still rolling the tape,

Hollow point smiles blocking the gate—

"Tell us what's next"

Autograph for a fan

I don't even know who I really am—

I practiced my smile a hundred times

You even believed when I said I was fine

Missing Person

Delicate mess of wires
Tangled and rooting

Sirens blaring
Urge to run

Fingers cool on bathroom tile
Empty smile
Clean the gun

Another Missing Person
Angel of Mercy
Comma Death

Delicate mess of a tortured soul
Finally laid to rest

Pretty

She knew the executioner
He took her hand with pride

He led her to fermented fruit
And insisted that she tried

He reminded her of someone great
But made her feel so small

She tried to hear the warning pleas
But found she could not hear at all

He said it would be good for her
The first of many lies

She knew the executioner
thought she looked pretty
when she cried

Envy

A bird uncaged

who cannot sing

Each night she visits me

And sings her broken warbled tune

To taunt the bourgeoisie

And through her pitchy cries

I dote upon her sanity

A bird uncaged

Who cannot sing

Whom taunts the bourgeoisie

Simmer

Wicked weeds have sprouted in my garden

They have conspired with the morning sun

Beneath the ground a fluid notion

Of manic opus, yet to come

Little Brother

Covert omissions negating fact
Hid surreptitious truth

Concealing subdued petulance,
Well-tempered deceit
Disguising youth

Morally incompetent
Always needing more

Exhausted every resource
What are Little Brothers for?

Narcissistic flattery
A complex of divine

Hidden in the basement
His casket molded after mine

Amsterdam

Any piece
I'd pay to see
A coffee shop
In Amsterdam

Eccentric teas
The Common Thief
Entitlement be damned

Eerie glow
Of familiar road
Confessions be condemned

Only search
The darkest troves
When with your closest friend

Prophetic smoke
A cloud of hope
Indicative I am

Maladaptive living
Every night
In Amsterdam

Dark Wood

Reminiscent of the forest dark

Of gnarled roots embrace

Fall victim to the truths untold

By impotence and grace

To lay lament with circuit cries

While shallow water run

Reminiscent of the forest dark

And pyrrhic battles won

Kept

'Tis I who locks the gates of hell
Cloaked by the common tint of flame

I cannot see without my eyes
But with them I see blame

I've taken on my keeper's tasks
Though the time I have is borrowed

My keeper tasked with solitude
Accursed by solemn sorrow

And within the cage
Without my eyes
I heard as my keeper fell

And back to me
Returned my sight
As I locked the gates of hell

Twilight

Mercifully you wandered on
I feel you in the breeze

Your cloudy eyes a gentle blue
With painful sighs you'd plead

Brittle bones embroidered black
Worn by inherent pacing

Would you resent my choice to free you?
Like your ghost I'm facing

Auburn plumage in the fall
Husky coat deplores the weather

I imagine how we could have played
If we could have stayed together

Better?

Through each seasons change

Viewed a stagnating form

With salt 'neath her nails

Escape tempts forlorn

Now you must see her

She's hard to ignore

A remnant of beauty

She wasn't before

UnWelcome

Not a likable woman
Wanted everything in sight

Not always a stranger
Wanted nothing but the night

Finally—
My chains were broken
At their weakest link

My compression cracked chest
Freeing me from the clink

Retreating to the coven
Unwelcome, but allowed

When I recall the penitentiary
It mortifies the crowd

Perfectly Preserved—

Spot cleaned with vodka
Hanged to dry

Faith in my revolver

After being buried alive

There is nothing for me here
The great pretender makes you think

Oh, weren't you so lucky
To have broke your weakest link

Yellow Bicycle

I found a yellow bicycle
At a twenty-dollar sale

A couple parts were missing
Yellow paint was chipped and pale

Both tires had gone flat
We both had been ignored

I fixed that yellow bicycle
For three whole summers more

Replacing rusted metal
Piece by piece with chrome

One day I'll ride my bicycle
But fixing it's my home

Mother's Unforgettable Cry

Mother cries up in her bedroom
Though mother's only ten

She recites a line of poetry
Then Mother tries her cry again

From her window she will listen
To a little girl like her

The little girl reads poetry
And cries after the words

Such a tragic poem
Mother - Daughter fight

Daughter goes to party
Her Mother's dead by night

Now I recite my poetry
Under Mother's watchful eye

Mother's ever reminiscent
Of The Unforgettable Cry